study series workbook

skip ross

melody farrell

r.g. triplett

THIS BOOK IS PUBLISHED BY LOST POET PRESS

This is a compilation of writing by the three contributing authors, all based on the "Dynamic Living Seminar" by Skip Ross.

Text copyright © 2015 by Lost Poet Press

Graphic art copyright © 2015 by Lost Poet Press

All rights reserved.

Published in the United States by Lost Poet Press

First Edition

No part of this publication may be reproduced, stored in a retrieval system, or transmitted in any form or by any means, electronic, mechanical, photocopying, recording, or otherwise, without written permission from the publisher.

www.thrivestudy.com

www.lostpoetpress.com

ISBN 978-0-9914489-7-5

Printed in the U.S.A.

Lost Poet Press first edition printing, October 2015

a note from the authors

Foreword by Skip Ross

The adventure of life is indeed designed for you and me to THRIVE. I have not always understood that, and consequently I have not always believed it. When the realization that thriving is possible first invaded my conscious mind those many years ago, the belief was rather immediate. It is the understanding and application that have been a process. Fortunately for me, I got the first glimpse of this truth at a point of desperation in my life when total immersion in the study of the process was my only option. As a result, my belief level was profound, my initial change dramatic and my determination to persist in it for life was secured. I began to understand that my lack of perfection was not a reason to give up, but rather the personal motivation to continue on and pursue excellence in the joy of living.

In those early days, I was pretty much alone, and yet surrounded by the silent mentors I found in the books I read and the people I met. There were many — Glenn Bland, Charlie 'Tremendous' Jones, Claude Bristol, Norman Vincent Peale, Robert Parmenter, Zig Ziglar, Jim Rohn, a philosopher or two of the ancient past, and a host of inspired writers in the Scriptures. "Total immersion" for me became 3-5 hours a day, 7 days a week for 18 months. Life began to change as my thinking began to change. I believe I was the first to recognize the change, but it soon began to impact others. It was at this point that the realization of my life's purpose took form. I wanted to pass it on to as many people as possible, but more specifically to teenagers.

As the adventure has continued over these years I have been joined in my pursuit of excellence by a whole band of wonderful people. The fervent prayer of my loving mother, the total belief in me from Susan, my wife, the profound encouragement of my children, the undillidaliable support of Leadership Teams at Circle A, the enthusiastic participation of thousands of campers, and the empowering affirmation of friends and business associates around the globe have all contributed to who I am today.

Here is one of my major discoveries and inspirations: today I am not alone. There are still many more with the longing to join the journey, affirm the adventure, and THRIVE. The culmination of this project is the beginning of the next phase. It has become the affirmation and embodiment of something I began believing, then practicing, and then teaching, so many years ago. The ultimate dream and goal of one's life is never fully realized until after that person has passed on.

The dream, therefore, never loses its empowering, energizing impetus toward fulfillment. It continues to draw one forward to the next level. I am there. The people I love are there. Now you are here with us. Join us in this adventure called THRIVE. I can tell you that the intersection of this THRIVE study with your life is neither coincidental nor accidental. There is a greater purpose for us all. Now it is your choice. With all my heart, soul, and spirit I encourage you to make this a "total immersion" adventure. Discover and fall in love with the best you it is possible to become. You are a beautiful, wonderful, and totally unique creation and you deserve to live that way!

- Skip

Foreword by Melody Farrell

If you know much about me, you know that I have grown up around these principles my whole life. Skip is my dad, so I got to live behind the scenes, and to see firsthand the "real story" of an internationally acclaimed motivational speaker.

And I have to tell you, with all of the integrity that I possess: my dad is the real deal. What we see and hear from him as a speaker are the same things that I saw and heard from him as his daughter. I have sat through countless seminars, meetings, trainings, and recordings ... and I have seen the same truths lived out day after day in the privacy of our home. I have experienced the beautiful victories that have come to our family as the result of this way of living, and I have witnessed the agonizing defeats that also are a part of being willing to risk so greatly in life.

I wish I could say that being raised in such a positive, encouraging, uplifting environment was the single key to my being an instant success in life. I wish I could tell you that I am now and have always been at the pinnacle of greatness, balanced and driven and free. I wish I could tell you that I have mastered every piece of this study and everything else my dad has taught ... after all, I've had every opportunity to learn things the easy way.

The truth is that I cannot tell you any of those things about myself, because sometimes the greatest lessons of life can't be learned or fully understood until we have experienced some of the deepest pains. Victory cannot truly be savored without the taste of defeat still lingering in one's mouth; balance cannot be truly appreciated until one has been sent careening off a precipice a time or two. The act of breathing in the genuine aroma of joy means a whole lot more when one has also inhaled the pungent scent of despair.

And so, my friends, I am not so different than you are. I have taken my share of knocks, I have explored my way around other schools of thought, and I have rebelled (in my subtle and rather invisible way) against the truths that I am now so very eager to share with you as a part of THRIVE. The good news is that the truths ingrained in every piece of the THRIVE project are not fickle or variable like our human hearts can be ... they are constant. They are here for the learning, for the applying, for the grasping. These truths will be available to you throughout your life, ready to help guide you down a path to becoming the very best you that you were created to be.

I am grateful for the environment I grew up in, for the truths that I have been taught and the mentors that I have had. I know without a doubt that these principles can make a massive difference in our quality of and significance in life ... and so today, I invite you to join me in walking towards them once more. Wherever you are, whether you haven't made many mistakes just yet or whether you are drowning in the midst of your problems and pains ... THRIVE has something to offer you.

I must say that the process of putting all the pieces of THRIVE together alongside a brave few who dare to look at the world this way has been one of the most rewarding experiences of my life. This project is the culmination of so much heart and energy and excitement and hope and purpose that I can hardly put into words how eager I am to share it with you. I am so grateful for those who have contributed to this project, to be a part of changing the world for the better.

- Melody

a note from the authors

Foreword by R.G. Triplett

As an author, a storyteller, I am always looking for the creative threads in any world, fiction or otherwise, that can pull the seemingly random stories and standalone truths together with a solid and newly formed knot of connectivity. I get inspired by the beautiful idea that in every adventure and every chapter of a tale, truth exists for a greater purpose than its momentary significance.

I have never had the privilege of attending Circle A Ranch. I have never been afforded the opportunity to sit through one of Skip's full Dynamic Living seminars, nor have I traveled the world to see thousands of people fill arenas and auditoriums to hear him teach them about business and life.

But I have very much witnessed the thread of Skip's legacy join me in something greater than myself.

It is amazing to me the effect that a simple conviction can have on the world ... and it is even more amazing to me the effect of what this simple conviction has had on my own world.

I think that is the point though, right?

Any good leader of hearts understands that their platform is shortchanged or handcuffed if it is contingent on their lone ability to present from it, because any leader worth his salt knows that his time is always and ultimately limited. But the great leaders ... the great leaders do not run from this, nor do their convictions wane in the mortality of the moments. No, the great leaders instill their convictions in the hearts of those who will carry the excavated truths to a new audience, in a new way, and from a multitude of new and different platforms.

I am a recipient of the gratuitous nature of these truths. Before I heard them spoken, I felt their convictions firsthand. I have tasted and seen and shared and laughed and cried and thought—long and hard—as to the merit of this way of living, because I have seen it and felt it from those who had seen it and felt it.

And what I have found cannot be undone, no matter how much I might want to pull away from it in the moments of discouragement or confusion ... the knot is always sure. The truths of Skip's convictions are clearly tied to an even greater truth, and that truth will always make life worth living, no matter what the circumstances happen to be.

This idea of thriving is not unique to Skip, nor is it limited to his many platforms, nor even to this project that we have worked so tirelessly to share with you.

And that is precisely what makes it so beautiful.

A thriving life is always possible, is always waiting, is always looking to share its stories and its principles with the unconnected world around it, tying us together in a way of life that we never knew enough to dream about.

So my prayer for you is this: may you think about and chew on the words that Skip has to share with us, and as you do ... may you give them permission enough to change the way you see yourself and this life you've been given. Because my guess is that when you do, you will begin to change not only your life, but the lives of those around you too.

My friends and I are excited to share this with you. I can't wait to see the way that all of the threads and all of the stories are pulled together in the end.

- RG

introduction to *thrive*

As children, we have a great capacity to imagine the best about life. We believe that we are capable of winning. We think we are invincible to our opponents, and we are not afraid to risk dreaming and hoping that our deepest desires will become realities.

Somehow, as we grow and experience more of the world, we discover that our courage starts to become beaten, and bullied, and even destroyed. And as our belief falters, we can find ourselves forced into a mold that merely fits our environment, our duties, and our obligations.

Could it be that there is a better way to live?

THRIVE study series proposes that there is. In this series, we will discuss an approach to life that begins with personal responsibility, leads to an awakening of purpose and an acceptance of ourselves, and ends with joy, hope, and significance in life.

Here are some questions that you will engage as a part of THRIVE:

Why do you experience fear?

- Identify how fear and worry can destroy your dreams.
- Discover how to handle fear and build courage.

Are goals and dreams worth fighting for?

- Find out how to set goals effectively.
- Engage with timeless principles that will lead you on a path to success.

Is balance in life even possible?

- Set priorities in the many areas of life that demand your attention.
- Learn how to structure your goals to achieve stability.

Where does your self-image come from?

- Realize what has affected the picture you have of yourself.
- Acquire the tools to begin to change that picture for the better.

What if you are meant to THRIVE?

- No one can earn self-worth and no one has to deserve it.
- What you are working so hard to get, you've already got ... a self worth loving.

THRIVE study series will begin a journey towards the discovery of answers to some of these questions. When you finish this series, you may not have every piece of it mastered, but you'll be armed with information, encouraged with examples, and inspired by your own engagement with the material. You will have a path to follow, if you so choose it. You will have some action steps in mind and you will have some targets to move towards.

The journey that begins in these pages will certainly not end here. This series is an encouragement to begin a new chapter in the story of your life, whether you have studied this type of material a hundred times before or whether this is your first time to learn some of these ideas. Today you can begin fresh and start down a path of learning and growing and becoming all that you are created to be.

You are invited to THRIVE.

how to use this study guide

This study guide is written for use with the **THRIVE study series** cinematic videos and the training videos by **Skip Ross**. These videos can be accessed at www.thrivestudy.com.

After you complete the **GETTING STARTED** section of this book, you will be ready to begin the 7 session course of THRIVE. This material can be studied individually, in a small group, or even in a large seminar. The book is written to be flexible, based on how you intend to use the material and how quickly you would like to move through it. If you are reading this on your own, you can just go at your own pace, whatever makes sense for you. If you are doing this in a group, your instructor will have a guide that will help with how best to use the group's time most efficiently.

For each session, you'll want to read through the **INTRO** section, and then watch the cinematic video. After that, you'll have the chance to go through the **REVIEW** and **RESPOND** sections before you begin the **LEARN** section. During that time, you will either watch the training video with Skip Ross, or your facilitator will teach the material in person. After the training, you can finish with the **CONSIDER** and **INSPIRE** sections.

The **STORIES** section at the end of each session is an additional piece that will help you have a deeper understanding of the principles you have learned. It's one thing to read about them in theory, but it's another thing to hear the stories of how they have actually made a difference. You'll get a chance to read a story in each section, and you'll also get a chance to write your own.

However you choose to go through the material, just remember that you will get out of this study what you put into it. The questions are meant to be a framework for you to focus your thoughts, but none are mandatory. Use this book in a way that will be most inspiring and exciting for you. The hope is that at the end of the series, you will have many notes in the pages of this book so that you can begin to implement much of what you have learned.

Let's begin with a **GETTING STARTED** session to prepare you with a basic understanding of the material and get your mind focused on the right types of questions.

welcome

Here are some of the questions that you will engage during your time with the THRIVE study series:

joy
How can we "choose to be happy" when we are guaranteed to have problems? What is the true meaning of joy?

fear
Where do our fears and worries come from? Is taking action enough to conquer our anxiety, or is there something stronger that can overpower our fear?

balance
How do we live a well-adjusted life when there are so many worthwhile pursuits constantly demanding our attention?

vision
Is there a way to set and manage goals effectively that will aid in their successful completion?

persistence
How do we overcome the disappointments, detours, and distractions that we will encounter on our way to becoming what we are created to be?

image
If the way we see ourselves affects everything we do, then how do we begin to change that image into something better?

worth
How can we pull away from the broken system of comparison, competition, and blame? Is there a better way to define our worth?

getting started: *thrive*

respond

Which of these topics is the most interesting to you? Why?

_____

_____

_____

Which of these topics sounds like it will be the most challenging to you? Why?

_____

_____

_____

What is the main reason that you chose to be a part of the THRIVE study series? What do you hope to get out of this guide?

_____

_____

_____

learn

I am responsible.

It's an uncomfortable statement. It's one that many of us don't really want to believe. It's so much easier to blame our shortcomings or negative feelings on someone or something else.

But if we are truly going to become all that we are created to be, we need to pause for a moment ... because the truth is that we are the only ones who can be responsible for that becoming.

And that's exciting news! That means that the path to a healthier, more productive, more satisfying and significant way of life is only a decision away!

The tough part is... that decision is up to YOU.

The great part is... that decision is up to YOU.

 Watch the **GETTING STARTED video** with Skip Ross to learn a little bit about the history of THRIVE and about how you can best approach this study to get the most out of it.

getting started: *thrive*

consider

In the three spaces provided, think of the different sources or experiences that you have blamed for problems in your life. It may be people, it may be conditions, it may be circumstances. Whatever it is that you hold responsible for your lot in life, write them down.

▶ _____

▶ _____

▶ _____

Now, for the tough part. Think about what it would be like to release those things or people or experiences from the burden of having to make your life better. If you aren't dependent on those things to be responsible, then it's easier to shift your perspective and your attitude so that you can honestly say, with excitement and purpose:

"I am responsible."

session one

joy

intro

What *is* joy, anyway? Is it a response that is based simply on the circumstances of our lives? Is it a reaction to the good things that happen to us ... an effect of a satisfactory cause?

Or, is true joy something altogether different?

Watch the **JOY cinematic video**, and let's set the stage for our discussion on joy and happiness.

review

What is this joy and happiness thing really all about?

If we are guaranteed to have problems and promised to have difficulties, how is a life full of joy and happiness even possible? Is it even something worth considering and working towards? There are many who live their lives as though we are all are merely subject to the whim of fate. They believe that circumstances influence us to be happy in the good times and discouraged in the lousy times.

Perhaps there is a different way to look at joy and happiness. Perhaps happiness is not just for the select few that have an internal gift for seeing the good in everything. Real joy might be attainable for everyone, not just for those who are born with an attitude that naturally sees the glass half full.

Let us consider a different proposition: *true happiness and joy come as the result of something completely different: a choice.*

A choice to be happy ... regardless of circumstances.

Now, none of us wants to choose to parade around with fake, positive pretense, so if that's all we are talking about here, we might as well close our books and go home. However, we are talking about so much more. We are talking about a resting condition of our hearts that does not have a direct association with the circumstances we are dealt. And that resting condition is where we find a joy and happiness that cannot be faked or pretended. We find a joy and happiness that will instead change our lives forever.

respond

When is the last time you felt joy over something in your life?

_____
_____
_____

Write about a time that you allowed a circumstance to take away your happiness.

_____
_____
_____

Who is the most joyful person you know? What makes him or her joyful?

_____
_____
_____

When you feel happy, what do you most want to do?

_____
_____
_____

learn

If we lived a life with no problems, it would be easy to choose joy and happiness, right? Without any opposition, without any threat to our dreams or our safety or our passions, joy and happiness would be our resting state of being. We would be free to pursue our becoming without being hindered by our problems.

And so it seems that problems, challenges, and difficulties are what stand in the way of allowing us to choose joy and happiness every day.

So here is the good news: if we figure out what to do with our problems, they will no longer have the power to hold our joy and happiness hostage. We will be free to choose joy and happiness despite our circumstances, and that is most definitely a better way to live.

 Watch the **JOY teaching video** with Skip to learn a little more about problems and challenges.

joy

consider

List in the spaces provided 3 different problems that have arisen in your life over the past year. In the first space, write about a problem that came for the clear purpose of showing you what you were capable of becoming. In the second space, write about a problem that came as the result of a wrong choice. In the third space, write about a problem that came for a higher purpose.

▸ _____

▸ _____

▸ _____

Think about a problem in your life that is holding your joy and happiness hostage. Let's handle the problem.

    a. State the fact that there is a problem

    b. State the problem

    c. State the solution and take action

    d. Never talk about the problem again, only the solution

inspire

What is one takeaway action step that you can pull from this session about joy? When are you planning to implement it?

stories

Here's a story from Skip:

As a parent, I knew it was my responsibility to help my kids understand that happiness in life is a choice. The joy that we experience comes as result of the decisions that we make. The circumstances of life will vary. Sometimes they will be very good. Sometimes they will not be good at all. We cannot tailor the circumstances of our lives so that we never experience anything but good times.

I knew that one of the ways by which I could help my children to understand this is by living the kind of life that I was encouraging them to live. I also knew that repetition of these ideas is crucial to understanding and embracing them. So I began, when they were very young, to say to them over and over again, "You always have a choice. You can choose to be happy or you can choose to be grumpy. It's always better, it's always smarter, and it's always wiser to choose to be happy."

I was not sure how long it would take, nor whether it was even possible to get a young child to understand and believe in this approach to life. Imagine with me then, for just a moment, the excitement I felt one morning when I began to see the results of my efforts. I walked out of the bedroom one day and approached the kitchen, and as I did I heard someone talking. It was not immediately obvious exactly who it was that was speaking. I knew that Susan was still in the bedroom. As I gently walked toward the kitchen and peeked around the corner, I was surprised to see our two-year-old daughter, Melody, seated in her highchair at the kitchen table. She was talking to someone. I decided not to interrupt, but simply to go to the corner and listen.

As I looked around the corner I discovered that she was talking to four of her teddy bears. The teddy bears were neatly arranged in a semicircle in front of her on the kitchen table. Interestingly enough, she was obviously in the middle of teaching a seminar to the teddy bears. Somehow I knew this was going to be an exciting moment in her life and mine. I made the decision that instead of walking into the kitchen I would just stand there and listen to what she was saying to these tiny little creatures.

To my amazement, I heard her say to each of the teddy bears words that sounded very familiar to me. "Now Teddy, you always have a choice! You can choose to be happy or you can choose to be grumpy." With her arm raised and her pointer finger extended, she continued, "Now Teddy, it is always better, it is always wiser, it is always smarter to choose to be HAPPYYYYY!"

Well, on the word "happy", her arms shot up over her head in a joyful glee and the heart of her daddy almost jumped out of his chest!

Now, here's your chance to write your own story:

intro

Where does our fear come from? Why do some of us spend our whole lives controlled by fears, anxieties, and worries? Is there a way to be free from the paralyzing power of fear?

Watch the **FEAR cinematic video**, and let's set the stage for our discussion on fear and worry.

review

Fear. We all have it ... and yet most of the things that we fear on a day-to-day basis are not fears that we were born with. They are fears that have been acquired during our experience of life.

We do not wake up one day with anxieties and apprehensions that just *appeared* after years of being unafraid and confident. Our fear is built up, year after year, experience after experience. We either find a way to handle it, or we become a lesser version of ourselves because of it.

Some of us simply run away from fear, and never attempt anything that makes us afraid.

Sometimes we fight the fear, trying to force ourselves to be braver than the concerns that attempt to control our decisions. We take action to prove that we can overcome our fear. And sometimes, the action works, and we find courage as we face the thing that has paralyzed us for so long.

Then again ... sometimes the action fails miserably, because not all fears are unfounded.

So some of us have learned to dilute the presence of our storehouse of fear by overflowing it with the right kind of thinking. We stay away from the things and people that contribute to our anxiety and we embrace the things and people that fill our minds with healthier ideas and pursuits.

And while this helps to avoid adding to the reservoir of fear and worry that we all carry around between our ears, it doesn't completely conquer the underlying insecurities.

There is only one motivator that is stronger than fear.

It's love.

And love doesn't fear the loss of what we hold most dear. It doesn't worry over failure, and it isn't burdened with anxieties and doubts.

Love pulls us towards the completion of our passions and desires, because real love shapes us into becoming all that we were created to be.

It's risky to face our fears in a way that pursues the things that we love ... but in that pursuit, we might just find that our fear has finally been defeated once and for all.

respond

What are some specific fears that you worry about on a regular basis?

_____
_____
_____

Write about a time that fear stopped you from doing something that you really wanted to do.

_____
_____
_____

Who is the most courageous person you know? What makes him or her courageous?

_____
_____
_____

When you feel afraid, how do you usually handle that fear?

_____
_____
_____

learn

The truth is that most of the things we fear or worry about are little more than creations of our imagination. So many of us worry over what people think of us, or what mistakes we will make, or what hidden dangers lie in wait for us around an unforeseen corner in our future.

We recognize that the deepest desires of our hearts, the truest callings on our lives, hold within them the power to devastate us beyond repair. If we get what we most want, but then lose it, how will we survive? If we chase after a dream or a purpose, but fail in the pursuit, how will we cope with the disappointment? We fear loss so deeply that we never even muster the courage to try.

We fear failure, because we have bought into the lie that failure equals defeat. We forget that nearly every story of a dream achieved has countless chapters of failure before the success is ever attained.

We sometimes even fear success. We wonder what will happen to us if we actually succeed at all of the dreams and passions that are within us. We create scenarios where we fail at handling the success, or we begin to worry how we will balance our time and priorities. We convince ourselves that the risks are too great, and we give fear permission to steal our dreams.

But what we do not see, because we are so blinded by our fear, is that we are *already experiencing* the defeat and the devastation and the loss. When we allow fear to stop us from becoming all that we are created to be, we miss out on joy and purpose and passion. We walk away from relationships, give up on commitments, and pass by countless opportunities that could change our lives for the better.

There is a different way to live.

If we decide to conquer this issue of fear and worry, then we can live in the freedom of becoming the best versions of ourselves. We can live in the freedom to THRIVE.

Watch the **FEAR teaching video** with Skip to learn a little more about how to handle fear and worry.

consider

In the spaces provided, write about 3 different fears that you have battled over the past year. In the first space, write about a fear that you can handle with action. Write down what the action is that will conquer that fear. Decide when you will take that action, and put a date on it.

▸ _____

_____

In the second space, write about a fear that you can handle with dilution. Write down what specific positive influences need to take the place of the negative influences that are causing the fear.

▸ _____

_____

In the third space, write about a fear that can only be handled by choosing to be motivated by love rather than fear.

▸ _____

_____

inspire

What is one takeaway action step that you can pull from this session about fear? When are you planning to implement it?

stories

Here's a story from Skip:

I certainly remember some of the frightening experiences of my childhood that began to build the storehouse of fear that resides in the unconscious mind. The good news is that we can learn to respond in such a way as to overcome the debilitating, paralyzing effects of a life dominated by and founded upon fear.

I was standing in my office one day, looking out over the village green and paddock areas of Circle A Ranch, watching the final moments of one of our horsemanship classes. One of the younger campers was just finishing a ride with a celebratory air that seemed out of touch with the reality of the moment. I did not know the full story of the victory won in those moments until several months later.

Mary had arrived at camp with a profound fear of horses. Her first day in the ring did little to settle her feelings; in fact, the experience greatly enhanced her fear. Mary was given a pony by the name of Joy, who was our smallest and most gentle horse on the ranch ... most of the time. Though Joy was ordinarily very obedient, she must have sensed a deep fear in her rider that day. Joy decided she did not want to be giving rides anymore, and because she knew her rider had no control, she decided to lie down in the middle of the class with Mary still on her back!

Mary was frightened but uninjured, so she agreed to try again with the instructor walking alongside. They went around the arena four times, and Mary began to feel like she could do it alone. Joy walked calmly ahead until she was an appropriate distance away from the instructor ... and then she went down again! This happened two more times before they decided that perhaps Mary had had enough and that next time she came to class, she could ride another horse.

And here's the good news: Mary did. The small celebration I witnessed from my office that day was just after the next successful ride. Mary had faced her fears, chosen action in spite of them, and conquered them victoriously. The full understanding of the triumph over this fear in Mary's life came several months later when her father called me to announce he had just bought Mary her very own horse!

fear

Now, here's your chance to write your own story:

session three

balance

intro

Achievement and significance in life are worthwhile pursuits. They are what can bring us energy, passion, and excitement about the way we live. They can motivate us to be our best and they can inspire others around us.

Worthwhile goals are hugely important on the path to achievement and significance. If our dream is just an end-point, without a focused plan of measurable steps along the way, we usually won't get very far.

But before we can learn about setting and achieving these goals, we need to consider balance. We cannot embark on a quest to achieve our goals without first evaluating the cost of what it will take to get there. A life that wants to THRIVE will always seek to keep every goal or dream or pursuit in balance.

Watch the **BALANCE cinematic video**, and let's set the stage for our discussion.

review

Our society is busy. For most of us, there are far too many things asking for our attention. We spend our days constantly chasing to-do lists, fulfilling obligations, and pushing ourselves to our limits just to keep up with our hectic schedules.

Sometimes, in the busyness, we get so focused on a certain piece of our lives that it begins to hurt or destroy the other pieces. We want to master our physical health, so we commit to a rigorous schedule of workouts ... but in doing that we sacrifice time with our kids that we can never get back. Or maybe we want to excel in our workplace, get the promotion and the raise ... but in doing that we sacrifice our time with family and friends, our health, and our emotional well being. Or maybe we settle into the super-parent mentality, where every waking moment is spent obsessing over our children and how to give them the perfect experience of life ... but we end up sacrificing our adult time, our friendships, and maybe our own dreams of what we had hoped to achieve ourselves.

There are countless scenarios that could be presented, and all of us have experienced the tension that happens when our lives get thrown out of balance. There is a weariness that comes from pushing too hard in one or many areas of our life, but that is a weariness that can be avoided by choosing to be deliberate about balance and priorities.

Remember: our significance in life is not found in where we end up or what we achieve; it is found in *HOW* we choose to get there.

respond

What area of your life do you feel is most out of balance? Is it taking up too much or too little of your time and energy?

_____

_____

_____

Write about a time that you allowed an over-concentration in one area of your life to negatively affect another area.

_____

_____

_____

Who is the most balanced person you know? What makes him or her balanced?

_____

_____

_____

When you feel like things are in balance in your life, what do you most want to do?

_____

_____

_____

learn

The key is to be deliberate about balance. Find ways to prioritize your life and your time. Instead of allowing a focus on the area of your life that matters most to you to be something that DRAINS all the other areas... allow that focus to be something that FUELS all the other areas. Choose to see the truth that health in one area of life will equate to health in the other areas as well. Investing time into your emotional well-being will make you a better parent, a better employee, a better student. Investing time into your physical health will also aid in your emotional health, your relationships, and your job performance. Investing time with your family will certainly influence every other area for the better.

The principle of exclusion is another vital component of creating balance in your life. The idea is this: *get rid of what you don't want to make room for what you do want.* This can be applied to just about everything in your life. If you want new clothes in your closet, you'll need to get rid of the old ones first. If you want new habits in your routine, you'll need to get rid of the old ones first. If you want positive influences in your life, you'll need to get rid of the old ones first.

It is time to declare war on the negatives in your life. Be deliberate about what you allow to influence you. If books that you are reading or television that you are watching is causing you to have a negative perspective on life, consider replacing those practices with positive input. If friends that you associate with are persuading you to participate in gossip, negative conversation, or unhealthy activities, it may be time to disassociate with those people.

The most important place where you can practice this principle is in your own mind. How much of your day is filled with negative self-talk? How much time do you spend listening to your own critiques and discouragement of yourself? Decide today that you want to make room for something better in your mind.

When you practice the principle of exclusion, you will begin to achieve a life of balance. Unimportant commitments and negative input will be removed so that you can invest your time and your energy into the best pursuits. Weariness will be less and less of a problem when you can exclude the obligations and influences that directly contribute to the weariness.

Balance. Balance. Balance.

Let it be a theme in your mind and a commitment of your heart. Be purposeful about creating balance in your life, and be deliberate about taking the time to rest and appreciate the beauty along the way.

Watch the **BALANCE teaching video** with Skip to learn a little more about what a balanced life should look like.

consider

The spaces provided indicate 6 major areas of life: business, home, social, physical, mental, and spiritual. In each section, write down the roles that you play. What obligations do you have these areas? What passions do you have in these areas? Are any of the areas significantly out of balance?

▸ _____

▸ _____

▸ _____

▸ _____

▸ _____

▸ _____

The next 6 spaces represent the same 6 categories. Write down some things in each category that might be taking your time and attention away from becoming the best version of yourself. Are these some things that could excluded from your life?

▸ _____

▸ _____

▸ _____

▸ _____

▸ _____

▸ _____

inspire

What is one takeaway action step that you can pull from this session about balance? When are you planning to implement it?

stories

Here's a story from Skip:

A number of years ago I was invited to speak at a major function in Minneapolis, Minnesota. The organization wanted me to talk on the effect of attitude upon one's health and experience of life. They had also invited another guest speaker for the day. His topic was to speak on the effects of physical conditioning and proper nutrition upon one's health and experience of life. We were both confident in our ability to communicate effectively on these assigned topics. He spoke first, and then I followed with my presentation. The agenda then called for my new colleague to return to the stage for a "physical demonstration" of his talk. I took my seat in the front row. We waited for his entrance.

Now, it is important to know that when we were introduced earlier in the day, we looked pretty much the same. We both wore a suit and tie, we both were about 5'8" tall, we both weighed about 185 pounds. So I was not fully prepared for the demonstration that followed. You see, this man was a world-class bodybuilder who had won numerous titles including "Mr. North America."

He came on stage in an abbreviated version of a swimsuit that left little to one's imagination. People who were familiar with bodybuilding competition would not have been surprised. I was not familiar. I was surprised. Shocked might be a better word, because sitting next to me was my 16-year-old daughter who was traveling with me that weekend. Barely 15 feet in front of us is a virtually nude man and I am trying to figure out how to get out of there. About halfway through his routine, my daughter elbowed my side and said, "Dad, this is gross!" I quickly agreed.

The fact is, however, that it was the most impressive physical demonstration of muscular development I had ever seen. I was somewhat embarrassed, somewhat intimidated, but I was impressed. Later, we had lunch together. I told him what an extraordinary demonstration of physical ability that had been. I asked how long it had taken him to develop that kind of ability. He asked if I really wanted to know, and I assured him that I did.

He said, "For the last 10 years, 10 hours a day, seven days a week, I have been in the gym, pursuing the development of my physical ability."

Wow! I proceeded with a follow-up question. "When you consider all of the recognition, all of the encouragement, all of the trophies ... was it worth it?"

He looked at me and said, "I would give it all up if I could just have my wife and daughter back."

You see, in the headlong pursuit of the physical perfection of his life, he had given little attention to the family who needed him ... and they had left him. He had not pursued his goals with balance in mind, and the achievement of those goals ended up being a very bittersweet victory.

Now, here's your chance to write your own story:

session four

vision

intro

Now that we have learned about the opportunity we have to choose joy, the importance of handling our fear, and the value of creating balance in our lives, we can move on to an exciting and inspiring piece of the THRIVE study series – goal setting.

When you are ready to embrace the idea that you can become all that you were created to be, the next step is to begin to see what that "you" looks like. Once you can visualize what you want to become, you can take some specific steps to set some goals that will take you towards that becoming.

Watch the **VISION cinematic video**, and let's think a little bit about vision.

review

Dreams. Goals. Burning desires. We all have them.

When we're young, it's easier to find expression for these parts of our souls that are begging to be groomed and trained and fought for … begging to *become*. We aren't afraid to speak of them, hope for them, and think about them in a conscious and deliberate way.

And there is power in our thoughts. There is power in the way we choose to care for the young or reawakened dreams. We can encourage them with our words and the mental pictures we paint of them, we can light them with the blaze of our desires, or we can trample them with careless words and negative opinions.

So if our thoughts hold such power, what if we learn to **see** the fulfillment of our dreams before they even becomes realities? There is no better way to care for them than to get a clear mental picture of what we want, fill that picture with emotion, and HOLD ON to it.

A little creativity, a little imagination, maybe a touch of fantasy and a whole load of belief - and we can allow our mind and our heart to experience a world where **we have become** the person we dreamed we would be.

This process of visualization isn't the whole answer. It isn't the full scope of what it takes to achieve our dreams and to become what we were created to be. But it certainly is a piece of the puzzle – it's a part of the process that can bring energy and focus and hope to our journeys of becoming.

respond

What are some dreams that have been awakened in you?

_____

_____

_____

Write about a time that you allowed a dream or desire in your life to be defeated because it wasn't cared for properly.

_____

_____

_____

Who is someone you know that visualizes or imagines what it would be like to achieve his or her dreams? What are some attributes about that person that you would like to emulate?

_____

_____

_____

What is a dream that you can practice visualizing?

_____

_____

_____

learn

When you begin to picture and imagine what it will be like to become all that you are created to be, then it is time to set some specific goals about how to get there. The process is simple: decide what you want, define it clearly and specifically, and write it down.

There is a way to go about setting goals that will lead to a greater degree of success. The fact is that many tend to set goals backwards. They look at their past accomplishments and failures and use their past to assess their capacity in the future. This cannot be the most effective way to set goals, however, because it gives the past a limiting control on the future.

Instead, we must look at what we want to achieve and assess what it will take to get there. We must decide if we are willing to pay that price and then we must take action. This action has nothing to do with our past — it has only to do with what we are willing to do with our future.

Once you have decided what you are willing to pay the price for, then you can set goals accordingly. There are 4 attributes of a proper goal:

1. **It is written in the present, positive tense, as though it is already a reality**
   ("I am a published author", not "I want to be an author")

2. **It is as specific as you can make it**
   ("I own a 2016 Acura TL, black exterior, black leather interior, with the luxury package", not "I own a new car")

3. **It is personal to you, not based on the actions or decisions of anybody else**
   ("I have deep and meaningful friendships", not "Dave is my best friend")

4. **It is measureable**
   ("I weigh 120 pounds", not "I am skinny")

Watch the **VISION teaching video** with Skip to learn what to do with these goals once you have them.

consider

It's time to write down some goals! This doesn't have to be the final list that you read every morning and every night, because you might want to take some time to refine them. But begin here by simply writing down 10 things that you would like to achieve in the next year. Remember to make them in the present, positive tense, and remember to make them just about YOU and the effort that YOU can put in to achieve them. Make them specific, measurable, and succinct. And have some FUN!

▸ _____

▸ _____

▸ _____

▸ _____

▸ _____

▸ _____

▸ _____

▸ _____

▸ _____

▸ _____

inspire

What is one takeaway action step from this session that you can make TODAY?

stories

Here's a story from Skip:

As newlyweds, Susan and I enjoyed a trip to the beautiful Cypress Gardens in Winter Haven, Florida. We strolled through the grounds, enjoying the plants and wildlife, and then we came upon a southern plantation style home. Susan could hardly contain her excitement, and I discovered that a home like this, a white plantation with columns all along the front, was Susan's dream home. We found someone to take our picture in front of the home, and she put the picture up on our bedroom mirror. She kept the picture for many years, always on the mirror, a dream that she believed one day would become a reality.

One day, many years later, I pointed to the picture on the mirror and said, "We had best build that before the kids are grown and gone!"

Susan went into action. We hired architects and designers, and began to bring in the necessary team of people that would build this dream home on our ranch in Michigan. However, the architect couldn't seem to draw it quite correctly. Apparently the southern plantation style homes were not meant for Michigan and the harsh winters.

Susan didn't give up. She found an updated picture of a southern plantation in a magazine, and took the picture to the architect in the hopes that he could visualize just exactly what she wanted. She then placed that picture in her daily planner where she would see it many times a day, keeping the picture of the dream fresh. The architect never "got the picture", but it was indelibly imprinted in Susan's mind.

Over the next few months we rejected many design drawings. We were committed to the building of our new home, just as Susan pictured it. We discovered that the picture Susan had cut out of the magazine was a property called Twelve Oaks in Sarasota, Florida. We were headed to Florida for a business trip, so we scheduled an appointment to take pictures of the home in Sarasota so that we could help the architect get the exact picture of the dwelling we wanted from every view and perspective.

Well, we missed the appointment! But we did go house hunting. The next two weeks were spent looking at rentals and lease-to-buys, condos and single-family homes. We were all over South Florida and we did find another home that was a completely different style than what Susan had wanted. We made offers and counter offers on this home, thinking that since we had already leased the ranch house in anticipation of building our dream home, we would move to Florida for a year or so until our plantation home was finally built in Michigan.

As we were waiting for the owner to accept our final offer, Susan felt the dream and vision of the plantation home inspiring her imagination. One day she said, "I wonder what Twelve Oaks will sell for."

I said, "Let's find out!"

The next morning, a video tour of Twelve Oaks arrived by Fed-Ex, and the following day we were on a plane back to Florida for a live tour. Two months later we packed our personal belongings and office essentials and headed south again, ready to move into the exact dream home that Susan had cut out of a magazine. That was almost 20 years ago. Twelve Oaks is more beautiful today than it was that first day when we drove down that driveway, curving its way through Spanish-moss covered oaks to the massive columns and arched two-story entry way.

It reminds us every single day of the power and beauty of a clearly defined dream.

Now, here's your chance to write your own story:

session five

persistence

intro

We have now learned about joy, fear, balance, and vision. We have begun to handle some problems, we have untangled ourselves from some fears, and we have excluded some pieces of our lives that were throwing us out of balance. We then set some specific goals to move us along the path of success and significance in life.

But what happens when the wind gets knocked out of our sails? What happens when the simple and straightforward plans we have made in our THRIVE study find themselves out in the complicated harshness of the real world?

Watch the **PERSISTENCE cinematic video**, and let's think about it.

review

Persistence just might be the most important piece of this study. The fact is that all of these ideas and techniques and personal development processes will take a lifetime to master. During that lifetime, you will probably experience seasons where things flow easily, goals are achieved rapidly, and the path of your becoming seems clear and purposeful. Then again, you will also experience seasons where obstacles arise, plans fail, and the journey that seemed so well defined and inspiring suddenly becomes hazy and discouraging.

In those seasons of defeat, which can come even after you are far along on the path of your development, the principle of persistence is the one thing that can always pull you forward. It can keep you motivated to continue to make good choices in the midst of bad circumstances. It can keep you committed to the process even when the temporary conditions make you want to give up.

Persistence is a choice. Giving up is a choice. And every day of your life, you will have the opportunity to make that choice.

So never give up. Never give up on *you*.

persistence

respond

What is one area of your life where you see yourself being successfully persistent?

_____

_____

_____

Write about a time that you persisted through a difficult or discouraging period. How did the success feel after the season of persistence?

_____

_____

_____

Who is the most persistent person that you know? How does that attribute benefit him or her?

_____

_____

_____

What is something in your life that is absolutely worth persisting in?

_____

_____

_____

learn

There are some key principles that will help you to be persistent in your journey to THRIVE: faith, enthusiasm, and self-discipline.

The principle of faith is a key powerhouse to your level of persistence. The fact is that these principles will only work if you truly believe they will work. Simply going through the motions of goal-setting without a solid faith that the principles will make a difference for you will undercut every single forward stride that you attempt to make.

Faith, however, is not something that can be forced. It is something that can be inspired and learned and cultivated through a process of growth. When you begin to take steps down the path of personal development, you will find that your faith grows along with your confidence and your understanding and your maturity. And when your faith grows … you cannot help but be persistent. Your belief will always drive your action, every time.

The principle of enthusiasm is another huge factor in being persistent. Choosing enthusiasm generates energy. By simply deciding to have energy and excitement about a task or a goal, you will find yourself being fueled to find more joy and passion in the journey.

A great example of the principle of enthusiasm is physical exercise. When we begin a cardiovascular workout, we frequently have to force our bodies to put the energy and power into the moves. However, after a few minutes of forcing the energy, it begins to flow naturally. Most athletes will tell us that they have more energy for the second half of their cardio routines than they do for the first half. Energy creates energy. And energy is certainly required for persistence.

In order to truly be persistent, we must also embrace the principle of self-discipline: *Do what needs to be done when it ought to be done, whether you like it or not.* There is little else that needs to be said about this principle. It is a simple – yet life-changing – decision to commit to self-discipline.

Watch the **PERSISTENCE teaching video** with Skip to learn a little more about these powerful principles.

persistence

consider

Answer the following questions. These pieces of THRIVE are perhaps where you will want to focus your persistence.

What is the one piece of the THRIVE study so far that you have the most faith in? What do truly believe will work for you?

▸ _____

_____

What is the one piece of the THRIVE study so far that you are most enthusiastic about? What gets you inspired and motivated?

▸ _____

_____

What is the one piece of the THRIVE study so far that you will have to be the most self-disciplined about?

▸ _____

_____

inspire

What is one takeaway action step from this session that you can make TODAY?

stories

Here's a story from Skip:

Our good friends, Darrol and Judy, were obviously the kind of people who would make great parents. They loved children and had sought to start a family of their own for over 12 years. Doctors had finally told them they were unable to have children. But Darrol and Judy were unwilling to accept that statement as a statement of reality. They continued their disciplined pursuit of better health and new knowledge to make their dream a reality. There were more than a few who questioned how they could continue to believe in a possibility that the experts said was an impossibility.

You can perhaps then imagine the profound enthusiasm with which they received the news that Judy was expecting a child. It was a momentous day when little Trisha Ann was born. Darrol, a photographer by trade, began a pictorial history of her life. Every Tuesday for the first several years, Darrol took dozens if not hundreds of pictures of little Trisha Ann. Thousands of memories, permanently preserved. I know this, because I was privileged to see those albums of Trisha Ann on frequent occasions.

It is not difficult then to imagine the enthusiastic expectation that began building towards the capturing of the moment when Trisha Ann would take her first, unaided step. Darrol was certainly prepared. There were multiple cameras, lights, and audio recording equipment. This was a moment to remember.

As little Trisha Ann readied herself for the attempt, the media frenzy began. Trisha Ann pushed off with her back foot, shifting her body weight to the front foot so that she could then lift the back foot and set it forward, thus accomplishing her goal. The cameras were rolling and recording as the event was brought to a sudden halt! When Trisha Ann pushed off too hard with her back foot, she sent the headlong momentum of her little body too far forward. Trisha Ann came crashing to the floor.

You all know what happened next, don't you? Darrol shut off all recording equipment, walked over to his wonderful daughter and reached down to grab her by the seat of her diaper. He took her to her room, tossed her into the crib and said, "That's it kid! You had your chance to learn to walk."

Is that the way it happened? Of course not!

How long did Trisha Ann continue to try to learn to walk?

Until she walked.

How long do we continue to pursue our dreams? Until the first obstacle? Until the tenth ridicule? Until the hundredth opposition?

No.

UNTIL!

persistence

Now, here's your chance to write your own story:

session six

image

intro

Self-image is the multiplying factor of everything we have learned so far. Without a healthy picture of the person that we want to become, how can we hope to move towards that becoming?

Watch the **IMAGE cinematic video**, and let's set the stage for our discussion on proper self-image.

review

The cinematic content of this session beautifully sums up the heart of this lesson. There is a bold courage that must be born in order to really grasp the truths that we are discussing in this THRIVE series. There is an understanding that must be embraced: You can become the *best* version of yourself.

Once you truly believe that, then you can begin to look at what the best version of you might look like.

When we think about ourselves, a picture comes to mind. Both visually and descriptively, there is a way that we perceive ourselves. In order to begin to make that a healthier picture, we need to start by examining what has shaped our current picture of ourselves.

The experiences in your past make up most of what has formed the picture you have inside. Both failures and successes, kind praise and cruel discouragement, false perceptions and accurate observations ... they have all contributed to your self image. And here is what is so intriguing: the experiences of the past have not actually made you the way that you are. They have only made you *believe* that you are the way you are. But, because you believe that, and because you view yourself through the lens of those experiences – what you *believe* about yourself **becomes** what you actually are.

respond

What are five words that you believe define you as you are right now?

_____

_____

_____

Write about a time that you allowed someone else or something else to define you.

_____

_____

_____

Who is someone in your life who seems to have a healthy self-image? How does that appear to effect his or her life for the better?

_____

_____

_____

When you imagine the **best** version of you, what are five words you think of?

_____

_____

_____

learn

Why is this self-image thing really so important? Couldn't it be that by implementing all the principles we have learned about, and by embracing joy and defeating fear, and by setting and achieving balanced and worthwhile goals, we will just become "better" people? Do we actually have to be deliberate about precisely what we want to be?

It is certainly true that all of the principles and ideas we have learned about up to this point have value that is inherent, a merit that isn't contingent on a proper self-image. However, the proper self-image is the multiplying factor. If we can get this part of our thinking correct, we can magnify and enhance every other piece of our personal development.

The fact is this – we will never act, for very long, in a manner that is inconsistent with the way we see ourselves. We will always be pulled back to behaving as the person that we believe we are.

So the question then becomes... can we change that picture? Can we start to actually believe the best about ourselves?

 Watch the **IMAGE teaching video** with Skip to learn a little more about how to create a proper self-image.

consider

In the space provided, begin to write about the person that you want to be. Think about people that you admire, think about virtues that you have seen in people from the past, and think about the times where you have seen the best parts of you shining through. Start the process of creating the description of the person that you want to be.

inspire

What is one takeaway action step that you can pull from this session about self-image? When are you planning to implement it?

stories

Here's a story from Skip:

It was my friend Zig Ziglar, who first said it so well. "You will never consistently perform in a manner that is inconsistent with the picture you have of yourself inside, the person you believe yourself to be."

My dad never went beyond the eighth grade in his formal education. He was self-educated, and he was a brilliant minister. He was not, however, a gifted mechanical engineer. In fact, around our home it was well known that Dad didn't fix anything that required the slightest mechanical ability to be fixed. As I grew up, I wanted to be like my dad. People often told me I was just like my dad. No one ever got very specific about those characteristics, and I never really stopped to deliberately consider how his lack of ability to work with his hands impacted me.

I do, however, remember one of my grade school teachers telling me to make sure that I never pursued a career that would require me to do any sort of work with my hands. It was a mistaken and very limiting piece of advice, an awful thing to say to a young, developing child. From time to time I made unsatisfying attempts to do things of a mechanical nature, which only confirmed and deepened the picture on the inside that I was not mechanically inclined.

In later years, when I began to learn the power of that picture on the inside and began to discover that I could actually change it, life took on dynamic new dimensions. I recall one day being at my brother's home when his 14-year-old son came in to announce that he could not mow the lawn because the lawn mower was broken. I immediately volunteered to fix it. The laughter from the family that accompanied my offer almost discouraged me from pursuing my newly emerging picture on the inside, but I determined to have a look at the mower.

David, my nephew, and I went to the garage. I proceeded to begin dismantling the lawnmower, looking for the problem. I found several things that didn't look quite right to me, so I cleaned and adjusted them as I went. Suddenly I realized the mower was in pieces on the garage floor.

I said, "Well that should do it. Now all we have to do is put it back together."

David said, "Have you ever put one back together?"

"No, but then I had never taken one apart until just now."

The moment of truth arrived when it was reassembled and I pulled the starter cord. When it roared to life I got so excited that I just had to test it out. I raced outside to the lawn as David ran after me. I mowed the entire lawn with David on the sidelines cheering me on. "Go, Uncle Skip! Go, Uncle Skip!"

Now, here's your chance to write your own story:

session seven

worth

intro

What makes you worth loving? Is it your looks, your charm, your talents and abilities? Or perhaps it's your success, your money and power and fame? How do you compare with friends, relatives, and associates?

Watch the **WORTH cinematic video**, and let's set the stage for our discussion on love.

review

We live in a society that influences us to find our worth in places that are fleeting. We find that the more we try to measure up to some sort of "successful" standard, the more we feel that we have fallen short. The competitive nature of everything that we do and accomplish makes us feel like no matter how far we come, we will never reach the standard that we are trying to meet.

We therefore begin to feel worthless. We begin to not only measure our own value based on these faulty standards, but we measure others' value that way as well. Money, power, fame, beauty, success, creativity, talent, recognition ... no matter how much we have, it never seems to be quite enough.

We then find ourselves facing two choices: either exhaust ourselves in an endless pursuit of attempting to be "good enough", or give up, and decide we aren't worth much of anything.

This system is broken.

If you could only take away one thing from this THRIVE study, the following understanding would be the most powerful piece of it all: *you can replace this system.*

worth

respond

What are some places where you feel like you don't measure up to what you wish you could be?

_____

_____

_____

Write about a time that you felt exhausted in the pursuit of being "good enough".

_____

_____

_____

Who is someone in your life that you frequently compare yourself to? What price has that comparison caused you to have to pay?

_____

_____

_____

What would it feel like to abandon this system of comparison and competition?

_____

_____

_____

learn

If we stick with this broken system of finding our value and worth by comparison and competition, we will never truly discover what it means to THRIVE. In fact, frequently when we are stuck in this system, we begin to rationalize that all the reasons we are not measuring up have to do with our being a victim of something or someone. We begin to blame the people and institutions that are closest to us: family, friends, work, church, school ... the list goes on.

When we get stuck in that pattern of rationalization and blame, we begin to lose touch with reality, with our values, and with the very relationships that make life worth living.

In order to THRIVE, we must abandon this system. Because here is the truth:

No one can buy or achieve success, happiness, self-sufficiency, immortality, or love. No one can earn self-worth and no one has to deserve it. Our self-worth is a given. What we have been working so hard to get, we've already got: a self worth loving.

Watch the **WORTH teaching video** with Skip to discover more about this new system.

consider

In the spaces provided, think about 3 areas of your life where you are the most prone to comparison and competition. Is it your looks, your professional standing, your academics, your creative accomplishments? Be as specific as possible. Once you have identified the 3 areas where you are most "stuck" in the old system, begin to think about ways that you can pursue excellence without having to compare and compete. Make some notes as to how you will begin to replace the system.

▸ _____

▸ _____

▸ _____

inspire

What is one takeaway action step that you can pull from this session about love? When are you planning to implement it?

stories

Here's a story from Skip:

I sometimes tell the true and incredible story of a boy we will call Charley (although that is not his real name). Charley was born with such a profoundly disfiguring and debilitating birth defect that his father disowned him at birth and refused to even have him brought home from the hospital. His family and friends followed suit, and Charley was treated as an outcast from the earliest days of his life.

What could possibly have engendered such revulsion and lack of love for a small baby? Charley was born with an exaggerated cleft palate birth defect. In fact, there was only an ugly, gaping hole in the center of his face where normally there would have been a nose and mouth and lips. Apparently it was so shocking and so painful to look upon that there was no one in his early life that would express the slightest affection, acceptance or love. Charley was abandoned, and he bounced from one foster family or institution to another for short periods of time. When he turned old enough to enter school, he was ridiculed and shunned by virtually everyone. He became an angry and violent young person, scrounging for food wherever he could find it and getting into trouble almost continually.

One day, a woman took compassion upon him. There was a depth of love and acceptance for Charley that could only be described as transforming and divinely inspired. Taking Charley into her home, she began to love him and accept him, regardless of his looks or his behavior. Those early days were difficult on both sides. Charley, rebellious and without trust or hope, violently refused many of the woman's attempts to help. She, devastated on many occasions by his rejection, began wondering if her love for him would ever be sufficient to change Charley's life. Finally, however, he began to accept her love, and her belief that he was worth loving. He allowed her to pay for a series of surgeries that began to restore most of his ability to function physically, and eventually created a facial appearance that was almost normal.

Then, Charley discovered that he could sing. He began to understand the universal languages of music and love. This opened the door of outreach to other rejected and hopeless people of all ages. Some years later, he returned to his home, community and family. His arrival into these lives brought a lesson of love and forgiveness that no one could escape or deny.

Charley's was a life transformed by love, and his life intersected mine when I invited him to come share his story at Circle A Ranch. Upon hearing his story and seeing his passion for spreading hope to the hopeless and rejected, my life too was transformed by the continuing thread of love woven into his life by a stranger, a woman who was, and continues to be, relatively unknown.

Now, here's your chance to write your own story:

conclusion

This is not the end of THRIVE.  This is only the beginning.

And here is what we need to remember as we begin to apply what we have learned and move forward towards becoming the people that we are created to be: *Personal growth is far more about the deliberate process of engaging each day than it will ever be about a final result.*

We can learn all of these principles—we can memorize the definitions and quote the experts and even make significant strides in our own lives to example the best of ourselves—but on any given day, for a wide variety of reasons, we can find it easy to forget it all.

If we do not continually engage on a daily basis with the type of thinking and reading and socializing and dreaming and purposeful decision-making that leads us towards personal growth, we will deteriorate. It is not enough to know these principles. Our task is not merely to learn material ... our task is to choose daily to participate in our own growth.

So, we must be patient. We must recognize that our becoming is about the journey. Most importantly, we must remember that if we fall away or forget to participate in our own growth, we can always come back. Every day is a new day – and we have a lifetime to work on it.

You have been invited to walk a path that will lead you to becoming the best version of yourself. You have been encouraged to live a life of joy, one that is free of fear and worry. You have been challenged to find balance in life by excluding the things that do not add value to you and your family and your dreams. You have been equipped to set effective goals and to pursue them with vision and clarity. You have been reminded to persist through challenges by choosing to practice faith, enthusiasm, and self-discipline. You have been given an opportunity to create a picture of the person you want to become. Most of all, you have been taught that this journey to becoming needs to start with the understanding that you are already worth loving.

You have been invited to THRIVE.

skip ross

Skip Ross is the owner, founder, and director of Circle A Ranch. He and his wife, Susan, have dedicated their lives to making a difference through this ministry, and have spent the last 37 years giving their summers to the work of Circle A. Skip is the author of several books and is best known for the Dynamic Living Seminar. He has traveled the globe teaching the principles of attitude development and leadership to millions of people for over 50 years. He is a successful business executive, recording artist, and motivational speaker. He is founder and president of the OFIDA Project, board member of Hansen Corporation, a Crown IBO with Amway, and a graduate of Westmont College and Fuller Theological Seminary.

melody farrell

Melody Farrell co-owns and operates a production company, Echo Media Group, and a publishing company, Lost Poet Press. She is associate director of Circle A Ranch and has held numerous leadership positions in various churches and ministries throughout her life. She, along with her husband Chris, was on the founding launch team of Element Church in Tampa, Florida, and currently serves as their Administrative Pastor. She holds a degree from Lee University and she operates a successful Amway business. She is a podcaster, a vocalist, and a mother of two. Skip is Melody's father, so she has been inspired and influenced by the heart of Dynamic Living for all of her life.

r.g. triplett

Bobby, as his friends call him, is an artist at heart. He is a professional musician and author - not to mention a private chef, daddy of two, and self-proclaimed nerd. He is a church planter, and has served as Lead Pastor and Worship Pastor in several churches throughout his career, having earned his degree from Palm Beach Atlantic University. He is co-owner and founder of Lost Poet Press, and he is also the on-screen narrator for all of the THRIVE cinematic films. He is the author of the Epic of Haven Trilogy, an allegory/fantasy saga that expresses his passion for grand stories and his rather epic view of the world.